EXPLORING COUNTRIES

Malaysia

by Lisa Owings

BLASTOFF! READERS

5

BELLWETHER MEDIA · MINNEAPOLIS, MN

Note to Librarians, Teachers, and Parents:

Blastoff! Readers are carefully developed by literacy experts and combine standards-based content with developmentally appropriate text.

Level 1 provides the most support through repetition of high-frequency words, light text, predictable sentence patterns, and strong visual support.

Level 2 offers early readers a bit more challenge through varied simple sentences, increased text load, and less repetition of high-frequency words.

Level 3 advances early-fluent readers toward fluency through increased text and concept load, less reliance on visuals, longer sentences, and more literary language.

Level 4 builds reading stamina by providing more text per page, increased use of punctuation, greater variation in sentence patterns, and increasingly challenging vocabulary.

Level 5 encourages children to move from "learning to read" to "reading to learn" by providing even more text, varied writing styles, and less familiar topics.

Whichever book is right for your reader, Blastoff! Readers are the perfect books to build confidence and encourage a love of reading that will last a lifetime!

This edition first published in 2014 by Bellwether Media, Inc.

No part of this publication may be reproduced in whole or in part without written permission of the publisher. For information regarding permission, write to Bellwether Media, Inc., Attention: Permissions Department, 5357 Penn Avenue South, Minneapolis, MN 55419.

Library of Congress Cataloging-in-Publication Data

Owings, Lisa, author.
  Malaysia / by Lisa Owings.
      pages cm. – (Blastoff! Readers: Exploring Countries)
  Summary: "Developed by literacy experts for students in grades three through seven, this book introduces young readers to the geography and culture of Malaysia"– Provided by publisher.
  Includes bibliographical references and index.
  ISBN 978-1-62617-068-1 (hardcover : alk. paper)
  1. Malaysia–Juvenile literature. I. Title.
  DS592.O95 2014
  959.5–dc23

                                                        2013034261

Printed in the United States of America, North Mankato, MN.

Contents

Thailand

Malaysia

South China Sea

Brunei

Kuala
Lumpur

Singapore

Strait of
Malacca

Indonesia

Indonesia

N
W   E
S

Did you know?
East Malaysia is larger than
Peninsular Malaysia, but most
Malaysians live on the peninsula.

Malaysia is a **tropical** country in Southeast Asia. Its two separate regions lie about 400 miles (640 kilometers) apart across the South China Sea. The western region is Peninsular Malaysia. It sits on the Malay **Peninsula**. Thailand is its neighbor to the north. To the south lies the small island nation of Singapore. Southwest across the **Strait** of Malacca is part of Indonesia. Kuala Lumpur is the capital city of Malaysia. It stands just inland from the western coast.

East Malaysia shares the island of Borneo with two other countries. The southern part of the island belongs to Indonesia. Brunei lies on Borneo's northern coast. East Malaysia surrounds the tiny country.

Mount Kinabalu

Did you know?
Mount Kinabalu is the highest point in Malaysia at 13,455 feet (4,100 meters).

Rain forests flourish in Malaysia's hot, wet weather. Their green covers the country's mountain slopes. Tall peaks run north to south down the center of Peninsular Malaysia. West of the mountains, the land flattens into a coastal **plain**. The eastern coast is more rugged. Narrow beaches break up the thickly forested mountains along the South China Sea.

East Malaysia's coastline stretches for about 1,620 miles (2,607 kilometers). Parts of the coast are lined with sandy beaches. Dense jungle covers the rest of the land. Green hills rise into steep mountains along the border with Indonesia. Rain feeds the Rajang and other rivers that flow down from the mountains.

fun fact

Heavy winds and rains visit Malaysia each year during the monsoon season. The season lasts from November to March in the northeast and from June to September in the southwest.

The island of Sipadan sits just off the eastern coast of East Malaysia. Its small oval of jungle is ringed by sand beaches. However, the real wonder of Sipadan lies beneath the ocean. The island is fringed with stunning **coral reefs**. They surround the undersea **volcano** that lies beneath Sipadan. These delicate structures transform the island into an undersea paradise.

Off the northern tip of the island, sharp-toothed barracudas swirl in tornado formations. Manta rays and hammerhead sharks swim close to the reef wall off Sipadan's southern coast. The reefs to the west are known for their softly waving **corals** and colorful fish. Green and hawksbill sea turtles are often spotted visiting the reef.

Did you know?

Sipadan attracts scuba divers from all over the world, but dive resorts are no longer allowed on the island. The government banned them in 2004 to protect the reef.

fun fact

One of the most popular dive sites around Sipadan is Turtle Cavern. This spooky underwater cave is filled with the skeletons of sea turtles that could not find their way out!

Malayan
tiger

Malaysia is known for its **diverse** wildlife. Elephants thunder through the forests of the peninsula. The patterned coats of Malayan tigers and pig-like tapirs help them blend into their surroundings. Huge monitor lizards sun themselves on the sand. Beaches on the peninsula's eastern coast attract sea turtles. Female turtles crawl ashore at night to lay their eggs.

hornbill

proboscis monkey

rafflesia

! **fun fact**
Malaysian rain forests are home to the largest flower on Earth. The rafflesia measures up to 3 feet (1 meter) across and gives off the scent of dead flesh.

East Malaysia is even wilder. **Endangered** orangutans and long-nosed proboscis monkeys swing through the trees. Flying snakes glide from branch to branch by flattening their bodies and swimming through the air. Hornbills and Bornean bristleheads wing overhead. At night, sun bears stick their long tongues into bees' nests to draw out honey. A few Sumatran rhinoceroses survive in protected areas across Malaysia.

Did you know?

Muslim men and women often cover their heads to show modesty and respect. Men wear black caps, especially on Fridays when attending prayer services. Women wear long scarves of all colors.

Almost 30 million people call Malaysia home. Most of them live in Peninsular Malaysia. About half of Malaysians are Malay. Their **ancestors** lived on and around the Malay Peninsula. Smaller groups of **native** peoples include the Ibans, Bidayuhs, and Kadazans. Other Malaysians came from elsewhere in Asia. The largest **immigrant** groups are Chinese and Indian. Around one out of every four Malaysians is Chinese.

Most Malaysians speak the country's official language, Bahasa Malaysia. English is commonly spoken, as are Chinese and Indian languages. Islam is the official religion. About six out of every ten Malaysians are Muslims. Other Malaysians practice Buddhism, Christianity, or Hinduism.

Speak Bahasa Malaysia!

English	Bahasa Malaysia	How to say it
hello	apa khabar	AH-pah kah-BAHR
good-bye	selamat tinggal	seh-LAH-maht teen-GAHL
yes	ya	yah
no	tidak	tee-DAHK
please	sila	SEE-lah
thank you	terima kasih	teh-REE-mah KAH-see
friend	kawan	kah-WAHN

Most Malaysians live in the bustling cities of Peninsular Malaysia. They prefer modern houses or apartments. Some live in shacks until they can afford a better home. Wealthy Malaysians drive cars from place to place. Others ride motorcycles. People in cities shop at large malls or vibrant outdoor markets.

Life is different in Malaysia's countryside. Most people there live in *kampongs*, or villages. Village homes in Peninsular Malaysia are built on **stilts**. Some have roofs made of woven palms. In East Malaysia, multiple families live together in large dwellings called longhouses. People buy goods in small local shops. Near rivers, sellers bring their goods in boats from village to village.

Where People Live in Malaysia

countryside 27.2%

cities 72.8%

Did you know?

Most Malaysian schools teach in the official language of Bahasa Malaysia. However, some Chinese and Indian students go to schools that teach in their native languages.

Malaysian children start school between the ages of 6 and 7. They attend primary school for six years. All students learn Bahasa Malaysia, English, math, history, and science. At the end of primary school, students take a test. Those who do well can move on to secondary school.

Most Malaysians attend secondary school for at least three years. After that, some move on to schools that teach them how to do specific jobs. Others continue in secondary school for two or more years. Graduates can apply for college in Malaysia or overseas. Many attend the University of Malaya in Kuala Lumpur.

Where People Work
in Malaysia

manufacturing 36%

services 53%

farming 11%

Malaysia is rich in **natural resources**. Beneath its soils lie tin, copper, oil, and natural gas. Some Malaysian workers dig these materials out of the earth. Farmers grow rice, rubber trees, and oil palms where there is **fertile** soil. Other trees are harvested for wood. Many of these resources are shipped to nearby countries.

In the seas around Malaysia, fishers fill their nets. Factory workers in Kuala Lumpur make medicines, electronics, clothing, and cars. About half of Malaysians have **service jobs**. Many work for the government. Others transport goods or work in shops. Those who work in hotels and restaurants serve visitors from all over Asia.

sepak takraw

Malaysians enjoy **traditional** activities and those popular all over the world. Top-spinning, or *main gasing*, is a favorite game. Players compete to see who can spin his or her top the longest. Another traditional sport is *sepak takraw*. Similar to volleyball, players have to keep the ball in the air. They can use anything but their hands. The most popular sport is soccer. Malaysians also enjoy badminton, cricket, and rugby.

Some Malaysians practice the **martial art** *silat* with knives or sticks. Quick thinkers enjoy the game *congkak*. They move pebbles or seeds around a wooden board. Malaysians also love to shop, go out to eat, and visit friends.

Did you know?

Shadow puppet plays called *wayang kulit* are a traditional form of theater in Malaysia. Performances usually carry on late into the night.

Did you know?

Most Malaysians eat with their right hand instead of using silverware. Chinese Malaysians use chopsticks.

A variety of Malay, Chinese, and Indian foods come together in Malaysia. Rice is a **staple** across all groups. It is flavored with coconut milk in the Malayan dish *nasi lemak*. Coconut milk also adds richness to spicy Indian curries. These dishes are made with chicken or fish and served over rice. Pork is used in *bak kut teh*, a Chinese stew served with rice and hot tea.

Char kway teow is a street-food specialty. Stir-fried rice noodles are tossed with fresh shellfish. Fried snacks are favorites at every market. Meat-filled pastries are sold alongside deep-fried bananas and sweet potatoes. A favorite dessert is *cendol*. This shaved ice is sweetened with coconut milk and green noodles.

fun fact

The Chinese dish of bird's nest soup is a rare treat in Malaysia. The nests are made from the spit of small birds that live in caves.

nasi lemak

bird's nest soup

Did you know?
Buddhist Malaysians celebrate *Hari Wesak* in spring. They release caged birds to honor the life of the Buddha.

Hari Wesak parade

Chinese New Year

Different groups of Malaysians celebrate different holidays. The most important holiday for Muslims is Ramadan. It is a holy month of **fasting**. *Hari Raya Puasa* marks the end of Ramadan with a feast. In the fall, Hindu Malaysians look forward to *Deepavali*, the Festival of Lights. Lamps and candles light up homes and float along rivers. The feasts and celebrations last for five days.

During Chinese New Year, the streets are filled with people and parades. Dragon dances are a highlight of the celebration. All Malaysians celebrate their country's independence with parades and fireworks on August 31.

Did you know?

Most Malaysian kites have a device on the front that vibrates in the wind. It makes a humming sound as the kite glides through the air.

Malaysia's skies are often decorated with beautiful kites called *wau*. Traditional *wau* frames are made of bamboo. For the sails, kite makers cut vine-and-flower designs out of colored paper. Some of the most common *wau* styles are *wau bulan*, the moon kite, and *wau kucing*, the cat kite.

Kite makers show off their best *wau* at festivals. One of the biggest in the world takes place in Pasir Gudang. Kites are judged on their beauty and how high they fly. Kite fliers take pride in their ability to make their kites swirl and soar. Smaller kites can loop and dive with slight motions of the hand. These graceful *wau* are symbols of the beauty and diversity of Malaysia.

Fast Facts About Malaysia

Malaysia's Flag

Malaysia's flag has fourteen red and white stripes and a fourteen-pointed yellow star. These represent the nation's fourteen states. The yellow crescent that sits next to the star on a backdrop of blue represents Islam. Yellow is the color of royalty. The country adopted this flag in 1963.

Official Name: Malaysia

Area: 127,355 square miles (329,847 square kilometers); Malaysia is the 67th largest country in the world.

Capital City:	Kuala Lumpur
Important Cities:	Klang, Johor Bahru
Population:	29,628,392 (July 2013)
Official Language:	Bahasa Malaysia
National Holiday:	Independence Day (August 31)
Religions:	Muslim (60.4%), Buddhist (19.2%), Christian (9.1%), Hindu (6.3%), Confucianism, Taoism, other traditional Chinese religions (2.6%), other or unknown (1.6%), none (0.8%)
Major Industries:	services, mining, manufacturing, farming, forestry, fishing
Natural Resources:	tin, copper, iron ore, oil, natural gas, timber, bauxite
Manufactured Products:	medicines, electronics, textiles, cars, steel, wood products
Farm Products:	rubber, palm oil, rice, timber, cocoa beans
Unit of Money:	Ringgit; the ringgit is divided into 100 sen.

Glossary

ancestors—relatives who lived long ago

coral reefs—structures made of coral that usually grow in shallow seawater

corals—small ocean animals whose skeletons make up coral reefs

diverse—made up of many different types or coming from many different backgrounds

endangered—at risk of becoming extinct

fasting—choosing not to eat

fertile—able to support growth

immigrant—a person who leaves one country to live in another country

martial art—a style or technique of fighting and self-defense

native—originally from a specific place

natural resources—materials in the earth that are taken out and used to make products or fuel

peninsula—a section of land that extends out from a larger piece of land and is almost completely surrounded by water

plain—a large area of flat land

rain forests—thick, green forests that receive a lot of rain

service jobs—jobs that perform tasks for people or businesses

staple—a widely used food or other item

stilts—poles used to raise a person or structure above the ground

strait—a narrow stretch of water that connects two larger bodies of water

traditional—relating to a custom, idea, or belief handed down from one generation to the next

tropical—part of the tropics; the tropics is a hot, rainy region near the equator.

volcano—a hole in the earth; when a volcano erupts, hot, melted rock called lava shoots out.

To Learn More

AT THE LIBRARY

Bankston, John. *We Visit Malaysia*. Hockessin, Del.:
Mitchell Lane Publishers, 2013.

Lyons, Kay. *Malaysian Children's Favourite Stories*.
Boston, Mass.: Tuttle Pub., 2004.

Weil, Ann. *Meet Our New Student from Malaysia*.
Hockessin, Del.: Mitchell Lane Publishers, 2009.

ON THE WEB

Learning more about Malaysia
is as easy as 1, 2, 3.

1. Go to www.factsurfer.com.

2. Enter "Malaysia" into the search box.

3. Click the "Surf" button and you will see a list of
   related Web sites.

With factsurfer.com, finding more information is just
a click away.

Index

The images in this book are reproduced through the courtesy of: haveseen, front cover; Juriah Mosin, p. 6; Tupungato, p. 7; Enzo Baradel/ age fotostock/ SuperStock, pp. 8-9; WaterFrame/ Alamy, p. 9; Gilles Malo, pp. 10-11; tratong, p. 11 (top); BlueOrange Studio, p. 11 (middle); kkaplin, p. 11 (bottom); Hemis/ SuperStock, p. 12; Shahril KHMD, p. 14; Wei Ming, p. 15; BartCo, pp. 16-17; IlonaBudzbon, p. 18; Justin Guariglia/ age fotostock/ SuperStock, p. 19 (left); Perspectives/ Glow Images, p. 19 (right); Carlos Barria/ Reuters/ Newscom, p. 20; Shamleen, p. 21; Kevin Miller/ Getty Images, p. 22; szefei, p. 23 (top); zhang kan, p. 23 (bottom); Calvin Chan, p. 24; sydeen, p. 25; Stock Connection/ SuperStock, p. 26; Ahmad Faizal Yahya, p. 27; Maisei Raman, p. 28; Vladimir Wrangel, p. 29 (top); melisamok, p. 29 (bottom).

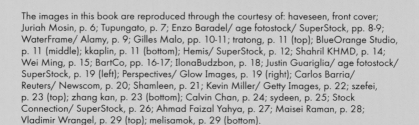